Crockpot Cooking for 2:

Easy Dump and Go!

Fix-It and Forget-It Recipes

By:

Mary Criswell-Carpenter

This book is dedicated to Marvin,

who has bravely tested my recipes for flavor and completeness,

especially the desserts.

Other Books by Mary Criswell-Carpenter on Amazon

Fiction

Maggie and the Stubborn Swede

Mary and the Marauding Indians

Katy and the Wolves at the Door

Non-Fiction

Chihuahuas

Turmeric

Polycystic Ovarian Syndrome

Cookbooks

Low FODMAP: 88 Gut-Friendly Recipes

Introduction

Thank you for purchasing this book, **Crockpot Cooking for 2: Easy Dump and Go! Fix-It and Forget-It Recipes.** This book is written for the busy person that wants a hot meal on the table each night, but doesn't want to spend hours cooking and cleaning after a long and tiring day.

It doesn't matter if you are single or a couple, these recipes are made for two meals. You can share the meal with another, or share it with yourself by eating it for lunch later in the week. You will save time, money, and food by cooking these very easy to prepare meals that have simple but delicious ingredients.

I've divided the meals by main ingredient; all of the meals are to be cooked in a small crockpot. They are all to be covered while cooking. I tried to list that step in every recipe but I might have missed one.

Within this book you will find:

- Breakfast Dishes
- Appetizers
- Beef Main Dishes
- Chicken Main Dishes
- Pork Main Dishes
- Vegetarian Main Dishes
- Vegetable Side Dishes

- Desserts

Crockpot Cooking for 2: Easy Dump and Go! Fix-It and Forget-It Recipes is born of the challenge of cooking for two, plus the desire to not spend the rest of the night washing dishes. I hope you enjoy these recipes.

Table of Contents

Chapter 1   How Cooking for 2 Began

When my kids were growing up I bought everything in the giant economy size. The boys were like eating machines. My daughter nibbled and grazed, but ate small meals. The adults in the family were overweight and ate giant-sized portions also.

I had a family of 5, but cooked every day for 10 people. I had a 6-quart crockpot, a giant Dutch Oven, and the biggest George Foreman grill that was sold. I had multiple gallon sized containers for storage. I had huge dinner plates, chargers really, and 16 ounce drinking glasses.

Then the kids grew up and moved out.

I lost weight, my husband is a much smaller man, and our cooking needs changed to more appropriate portions. If I cook a pot of chicken and dumplings the size I did previously, my husband and I eat on it a week and then still freeze or dump some.

Dumping food, as in the garbage can, or throwing food into the frozen Hinterlands where it will stay never retrieved is something that pushes my buttons. I will not say I was ever dangerously hungry, but I heard enough Great Depression stories from those who lived those times that throwing away food makes me ashamed.

I realized that I had to learn a new way of cooking or I would continue in these shameful practices of being wasteful.

I bought a new tiny crockpot and a new tiny George. I bought an electric pressure cooker. I gave away the giant appliances to a young person with lots of kids and very little time. I learned to cook all over again with the following appliances:

- 2-quart crockpot, and a
- 1 ½ -quart crockpot.

All of the recipes in this book can be cooked with just these two items and a few spoons for stirring. There are no pre-browning, pre-baking, pre-anything instructions.

When I get ready to work in the morning, I have no time to cook before I start work, and no desire to cook when I am ready for dinner. I decided you were probably of the same mind. All of these recipes are "fix-it and forget-it" so that you can dump the ingredients into the cooker and come to dinner with a hot meal prepared. There are suggestions to add rice or a side dish, but many of the dishes are all in one meals.

I hope you enjoy the recipes. Please leave me feedback on Amazon if you do.

Mary Criswell-Carpenter

Chapter 2   Breakfast Recipes

Baked Cinnamon French Toast

Nutrition Information

Per Serving: 444 calories, 13g fat (7g saturated fat), 202mg cholesterol, 430mg sodium, 71g carbohydrate (44g sugars, 2g fiber), 14g protein

Ingredients

- 4 slices Cinnamon Swirl Bread or Raisin Bread
- 2 eggs
- 1 cup milk
- 2 teaspoons butter
- ½ teaspoon cinnamon
- 1/4 cup sugar
- *Optional, 1 teaspoon vanilla*

Directions

Cube the bread. Combine the eggs, milk, (vanilla) cinnamon and sugar in a deep bowl. Whisk until well blended. Place the bread into the egg mix. Butter the crockpot and have a nice cup of tea. Place all of the egg and bread mix into the crockpot. Cut the butter into small pieces and place on top. Cover, place a paper towel under the lid to catch the moisture, and cook for 8 hours. Will smell divine when you get up the next morning and taste even better.

Cheese, Eggs and Spinach Casserole

Nutrition Information

Per Serving: 450 calories, 30g fat (18g saturated fat), 243mg cholesterol, 848mg sodium, 11g carbohydrate (0g sugars, 1g fiber), 32g protein

Ingredients

- 1 cup cottage cheese
- 1 cup frozen chopped spinach, thawed and drained
- 2/3 cups shredded cheese, I like Swiss or Provolone
- 2 eggs, lightly beaten
- 2 Tablespoons flour
- 1/4 cup butter, melted
- 1 tablespoon finely chopped onion
- Liberal dash of salt

Topping

- Additional shredded cheese to top
- *Optional* Bacon crumbles

Directions

Combine all the ingredients into a bowl and stir until blended. Cook on High one hour. Reduce to low, cook 1 more hour until eggs are set and temperature is 160 degrees. Sprinkle with bacon and cheese. Cover until cheese is melted and serve.

Cherokee Hominy

Nutrition Information

Per Serving: 384 calories, 21g fat (6g saturated fat), 52mg cholesterol, 1445mg sodium, 26g carbohydrate (3g sugars, 5g fiber), 20g protein

Ingredients

- 1 drained can of hominy, any color
- 3 diced slices of bacon
- 1 Tablespoon black pepper
- 2 crisp slices of bacon, crumbled for garnish

Directions

Combine all ingredients, place in crockpot and cover, cook for 8 hours.

Serve with additional black pepper, and the crumbled bacon on top of the hominy.

Eggs and Sausage Casserole

Nutrition Information

Per Serving: 423 calories, 33g fat (13g saturated fat), 402mg cholesterol, 703mg sodium, 1g carbohydrate (0g sugars, 0g fiber), 28g protein

Ingredients

- 4 eggs
- 4 ounces cooked sausage or sausage crumbles
- 4 ounces cheddar cheese, shredded
- Salt and pepper
- ¼ cup shredded cheddar cheese for topping

Directions

Beat the eggs in a bowl, then fold in the cheddar cheese. Butter the crockpot. Pour ½ the egg mixture into the crockpot, salt and pepper. Pour all of the sausage crumbles over the layer of eggs. Add the other half of the eggs. Cover and place a paper towel under the lid to gather the condensation. Cook on low for 8 hours. Sprinkle with remaining cheese right before serving.

Serve with hot coffee, toast or biscuits and homemade jelly for a yummy breakfast.

French Ham and Eggs

Nutrition Information

1 serving: 315 calories, 18g fat (9g saturated fat), 256mg cholesterol, 942mg sodium, 17g carbohydrate (4g sugars, 1g fiber), 21g protein

Ingredients

- 2 large eggs
- 1/3 cup biscuit/baking mix
- 3 T milk
- 1/3 cup sour cream
- 1 T minced fresh parsley
- 1 garlic cloves, minced
- Dash of salt and pepper
- 1/3 cup cubed fully cooked ham
- 1/3 cup shredded Swiss cheese
- 3 T chopped onion
- 3 T shredded Parmesan cheese
- Dash of thyme

In a large bowl, whisk the first eight ingredients until blended; stir in remaining ingredients. Pour into a greased 1 ½-quart slow cooker.

Cover. Cook on high 1 hours then on low 1 hour or until eggs are set. Scoop onto a plate. Serve with fresh orange slices.

Maple Bread Pudding

Nutrition Information

1 serving: 284 calories, 8g fat (3g saturated fat), 176mg cholesterol, 206mg sodium, 40g carbohydrate (31g sugars, 1g fiber), 11g protein

Ingredients

2 cups bread cubes

1 cups whole milk

2 eggs

1 teaspoon vanilla extract

1 teaspoon cinnamon

1/4 cup real maple syrup

Directions

Whisk together eggs, milk, and flavorings. Pour over bread cubes in a buttered crockpot. Let soak 15 minutes then stir a few times to assure the bread is well coated. Turn on the crockpot to low, Cover and cook for 8 hours.

Serve with maple syrup.

Oatmeal with Apples

Nutrition Information

1 cup: 340 calories, 13g fat (5g saturated fat), 20mg cholesterol, 225mg sodium, 51g carbohydrate (32g sugars, 3g fiber), 10g protein

Ingredients:

- 2 cups milk (whole)
- 1 cup old-fashioned oats (not instant or quick-cooking)
- 1 chopped peeled Honey-Crisp apple
- 1/2 cup raisins, if desired
- 1/4 cup packed brown sugar
- 1/4 cup chopped nuts (some like walnuts, I like pecans)
- 1 tablespoon butter, melted
- 1/2 teaspoon cinnamon
- Liberal dash of salt

Directions:

Coat the crock-pot with butter-flavored Pam. Place all ingredients in the crock-pot, cover, and cook on low for 2 hours.

Chapter 3 Appetizers

Appetizers are recipes that serve more than 2. I couldn't think of a way to have a party without inviting other people, and well, you have to feed them, don't you?

Barbecue Chicken Sliders

Nutrition Information

Per Serving: 180 calories, 3g fat (1g saturated fat), 20mg cholesterol, 629mg sodium, 30g carbohydrate (15g sugars, 1g fiber), 13g protein

18 servings

Ingredients

- 1 (24-ounce) package frozen grilled chicken breast strips
- 1 (18-ounce) jar barbecue sauce
- 1/2 large sweet onion, thinly sliced
- 3 tablespoons molasses
- 1 tablespoon hot sauce, optional
- 18 dinner rolls, split

Directions

Stir together everything but the dinner rolls and place into a greased slow cooker. Cover and cook on high for 2 ½ hours. Shred the chicken with a fork and place onto the rolls.

Serve with cole slaw, pickles and assorted cheeses.

Beefy Cream Cheese Dip

Nutrition Information

Per Serving: 250 calories, 14g fat (7g saturated fat), 37mg cholesterol, 149mg sodium, 27g carbohydrate (13g sugars, 4g fiber), 7g protein

16 servings

Ingredients

- 2 (8-ounce) packages cream cheese, softened
- 1 (8-ounce) container sour cream
- 1/4 cup milk
- 1/4 teaspoon garlic powder
- 1/4 teaspoon black pepper
- 1 (4.5-ounce) jar dried beef, chopped finely
- 1/2 cup TOTAL chopped green, yellow and red bell pepper
- 1/4 cup finely chopped onion
- 1/2 cup chopped pecans, to sprinkle on top of the dip
- *Optional, hot sauce*

Directions

Mix together the cheese, milk and sour cream with a mixer until softly blended. Add the spices and a few drops of hot sauce, if desired. Fold in the chopped beef and peppers and onion. Place in a greased crock pot. Cover and cook on low for 3 hours. Stir and sprinkle the top with pecans and serve with toasted bagel pieces or pita bread.

Buffalo Dip

Nutrition Information

Per Serving: 200 calories, 19g fat (12g saturated fat), 62mg cholesterol, 208mg sodium, 4g carbohydrate (0g sugars, 0g fiber), 2g protein

4 servings

Ingredients

- 1 8-oz brick cream cheese
- 1 package ranch dressing
- ¼ cup Frank's hot sauce (or your favorite)
- ¼ cup blue cheese crumbles

Directions

Combine in crockpot and cook on low for 2 hours, stir and serve with celery sticks and chicken fries.

Chex Mix

Nutrition Information

Per Serving: 205 calories, 10g fat (3g saturated fat), 8mg cholesterol, 379mg sodium, 25g carbohydrate (3g sugars, 3g fiber), 6g protein

16 servings

Ingredients

- 3 cups corn Chex
- 3 cups rice Chex
- 3 cups wheat Chex
- 2 cups pretzel sticks
- 1 cup peanuts or assorted nuts
- 1 ½ cups Cheez-Its Crackers
- 4 Tablespoons butter
- 2 Tablespoons Worcestershire sauce
- 1 ½ teaspoons seasoned salt
- ¾ teaspoons garlic powder
- ½ teaspoon onion powder
- ½ cup grated parmesan cheese

Directions

Combine the butter, Worcestershire sauce, seasoned salt, garlic and onion powder in a bowl and microwave for one minute. Stir until well combined. Place the Chex cereals, peanuts and crackers into a crock pot. Pour the sauce over the cereals as evenly as possible. Cover and turn the crock pot on low. Cook for one hour, then stir. Cover and cook for another hour, then stir. Cook for a third hour, then taste to assure crunchiness. Pour into a large bowl and add the parmesan cheese, evenly coating the mix. Serve.

Any variation on this mix is acceptable. Many times I've added cheerios, or granola, or raisins and M&M's, all is good.

Crab and Spinach Dip

Nutrition Information

Per Serving: 188 calories, 6g fat (1g saturated fat), 26mg cholesterol, 300mg sodium, 26g carbohydrate (1g sugars, 1g fiber), 9g protein

Serving size is ¼ cup

Ingredients

- 1 1/2 cups lump crabmeat, drained
- 1 cup shredded cheddar cheese
- ¾ cup ounces grated Parmesan cheese
- 1/2 cup milk
- 1/2 cup finely minced onion
- 1/2 cup mayonnaise
- 1 tablespoon sherry
- 1/2 teaspoon ground red pepper
- 2 garlic cloves, minced
- 2 cups chopped baby spinach, stems removed
- 1 (8-ounce) block cream cheese
- 1 cup sour cream
- 1 teaspoon lemon juice
- Chopped jalapeño peppers to taste

Directions

Combine all ingredients into a crockpot and cook on low for 2 hours. Stir and serve with tortilla chips or toast rounds.

Hot Artichoke and Spinach Dip

Nutrition Information

Per Serving: 146 calories, 12g fat (5g saturated fat), 25mg cholesterol, 257mg sodium, 6g carbohydrate (2g sugars, 1g fiber), 4g protein

16 servings

Ingredients

- 1 (14-ounce) can quartered artichoke hearts, drained and coarsely chopped
- 1 (10-ounce) package frozen chopped spinach, thawed, drained, and squeezed dry
- 1 (8-ounce) block of cream cheese, softened
- 1 (8-ounce) carton sour cream
- 3/4 cup grated Parmesan cheese
- 3/4 cup milk
- 1/2 cup diced onion
- 1/2 cup mayonnaise
- 1 tablespoon red wine vinegar
- 1/4 teaspoon freshly ground pepper
- 1 Tablespoon minced garlic
- 1 can drained and chopped water chestnuts

Directions

Combine all ingredients into a crockpot, stirring to blend the ingredients together. Cover and cook on low for 2 hours.

Parmesan Dip

Nutrition Information

Per Serving: 73 calories, 3g fat (1g saturated fat), 3mg cholesterol, 167mg sodium, 9g carbohydrate (0g sugars, 1g fiber), 2g protein

15 servings

Per serving of 1 piece of bread and 1 teaspoon of dip

Ingredients

- 1 1/3 cups mayonnaise
- 1 cup shredded parmesan cheese
- 1 cup finely chopped purple onion
- 1 tablespoon chopped fresh dill or dill relish
- 1 tablespoon lemon juice
- 1/4 teaspoon pepper

1 loaf sliced French bread, toasted if you prefer

Directions

Combine all the ingredients into the crockpot except the bread. Cover and cook on low for 2 hours. Stir before serving. Serve on French bread slices or toast

Richer than the Same Old Cheese Dip

Nutrition Information

Per Serving: 171 calories, 9g fat (5g saturated fat), 40mg cholesterol, 1027mg sodium, 9g carbohydrate (6g sugars, 0g fiber), 12g protein

16 servings

Ingredients

- 1/4 cup butter
- 1 small onion, chopped
- 1 (4-oz.) jar diced pimiento, drained
- 2 cans Rotel tomatoes, 1 mild and 1 spicy
- 1 cup cottage cheese
- 1 (32-ounce) block pasteurized prepared cheese product, cubed
- 1 (5-oz.) can evaporated milk

Directions

Place all ingredients into a blender and mix until smooth but not liquid. Place in a crock pot and cook on low for 2 hours, stirring every 30 minutes. Stir again before serving.

Serve with toasted pita bread.

Sweet and Spicy Chicken Wings

Per Serving: 133 calories, 7g fat (2g saturated fat), 54mg cholesterol, 126mg sodium, 10g carbohydrate (8g sugars, 0g fiber), 9g protein

12 Servings

Ingredients

- 12 chicken wings
- 1/2 cup maple syrup
- 1/2 cup hot sauce (as hot or spicy as you like)
- 1 Tablespoon minced garlic

Directions

Combine syrup and hot sauce into a zip top freezer bag, gallon sized. Place the wings into the bag and seal. Refrigerate for 8 hours, turning as often as you remember.

Drain the wings and place into a crock pot. Cook on Low for 4 hours.

Remove the wings gently from the crock pot. Place on a broiler pan until crispy, about 7 minutes.

Serve with blue cheese dressing and celery sticks for crunch.

Tamale Dip

Nutrition Information

Per Serving: 161 calories, 10g fat (2g saturated fat), 24mg cholesterol, 685mg sodium, 11g carbohydrate (3g sugars,12g fiber), 7g protein

16 servings

Ingredients

- 1 can tamales, wrappers removed
- 1 (16-ounce) brick processed cheese, with peppers
- 1 can chili without beans
- *Optional, 1 can green chilies*

Directions

Combine all ingredients in a crock pot, breaking the tamales into bite sized pieces with a fork. Cover and cook on low for 4 hours. Stir and serve with tortilla chips.

Chapter 4   Beef Main Dishes

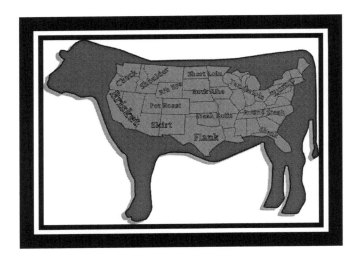

Baja Carne Asada

Nutrition Information

Per Serving: 605 calories, 33g fat (9g saturated fat), 125mg cholesterol, 715mg sodium, 9.5g carbohydrate (5g sugars, 0g fiber), 64g protein

Ingredients

- ¼ cup lime juice
- 4 Tablespoons minced garlic
- 1/4 cup orange juice
- 1/2 cup chopped fresh cilantro
- 2 Tablespoons olive oil
- 1 can chopped green chilies
- 1-pound flank steak
- Salt and pepper

Directions

Place all ingredients in the crockpot and cover, cook on low for 8 hours. Remove meat from crockpot and serve in tortillas, with sour cream and cheddar jack cheese.

Is excellent with Spanish rice and guacamole.

Beef Burgundy

Nutrition Information

Per Serving: 520 calories, 15g fat (5g saturated fat), 203mg cholesterol, 682mg sodium, 8g carbohydrate (3g sugars, 1g fiber), 73g protein

Ingredients

- 1 lb. beef stew meat, frozen
- 1 cup fresh mushroom slices
- ½ cup burgundy wine or grape juice
- 1 cup beef broth
- ½ cup pearl onions, halved
- 1 pkg. brown gravy mix

Directions

Combine all ingredients in a small crockpot. Cover and cook for 6-8 hours. Serve with green beans/Haricots Verts a la Provençale (recipe provided in the vegetable section) and buttered noodles.

Beef Stew for 2

Nutrition Information

Per Serving: 590 calories, 16g fat (6g saturated fat), 203mg cholesterol, 2096mg sodium, 30g carbohydrate (3g sugars, 2g fiber), 75g protein

Ingredients

- 1 lb. beef stew meat, frozen
- 1 cup baby carrots
- 1 cup potatoes, quartered, or more if you like potatoes a lot
- ¼ cup each, pearl onions and diced celery
- 1 ½ cups beef broth (or one can)
- 1 pkg. brown gravy mix
- 1 pkg. ranch dressing mix
- 1 pkg. Italian dressing mix
- ½ cup water
- Salt and pepper to taste

Directions

Place all ingredients in a small crock pot, with the vegetables on bottom. Place the meat on top and sprinkle with the seasoning mixes, then add the liquid. Cook, covered, on low for 6-8 hours. Serve with hot crusty bread.

Beef Stroganoff

Nutrition Information

Per Serving: 588 calories, 26g fat (13g saturated fat), 228mg cholesterol, 433mg sodium, 12g carbohydrate (6g sugars, 1g fiber), 72g protein

Ingredients

- 1 lbs. beef stew meat, frozen
- 1 cup fresh mushrooms
- ½ cup sour cream
- ½ cup onion, diced
- 2 Tablespoons ketchup
- 1 Tablespoon Worcestershire sauce
- 1 teaspoon minced garlic
- Dash of salt and pepper
- 1 Tablespoon corn starch for thickening

Directions

Combine all the ingredients except the corn starch and the sour cream into the crockpot. Cover and cook on low for 8 hours.

Before serving

Combine the corn starch with 1 tablespoon cold water to make a slurry. Mix until smooth, then stir into the hot stroganoff mixture. Stir until thickened. After the stroganoff has thickened, add the ½ cup sour cream. Serve over rice or noodles.

Chinese Beef and Broccoli

Nutrition Information

Per Serving: 679 calories, 12g fat (4g saturated fat), 204mg cholesterol, 410mg sodium, 49g carbohydrate (37g sugars, 2g fiber), 90g protein

Ingredients

- 1 lbs. fajita steak, frozen, already sliced
- ½ cup onion pieces
- 1 cup beef broth
- ½ cup soy sauce
- ½ cup brown sugar
- 1 Tablespoon minced garlic
- 1 small can water chestnuts, drained
- 1 Tablespoon cornstarch
- 1 cup frozen broccoli florets

Directions

Combine all ingredients but the cornstarch and the broccoli into the crockpot. Stir well to coat the beef evenly. Cover and cook on low for 6-8 hours.

Before serving:

Cook rice noodles or rice to serve with the broccoli dish. While the rice is cooking, add the broccoli to the crockpot and cover. This will cook the broccoli enough to thaw but still will have a crunchy texture.

Mix the cornstarch well with 1 Tablespoon COLD water. Pour the slurry into the crockpot and stir until thickened.

Serve over rice or noodles.

Hearty Beef and Barley Soup

Nutrition Information

Per Serving: 543 calories, 10g fat (4g saturated fat), 192mg cholesterol, 1895mg sodium, 31g carbohydrate (6g sugars, 7g fiber), 78g protein

Ingredients

- 1 lbs. cubed round steak
- ½ cup sliced carrots
- ½ cup diced fresh mushrooms
- 1 Tablespoon minced garlic
- 1 Tablespoon ketchup
- 3 cups beef broth
- ½ teaspoon thyme
- 1/3 cup barley, not the quick cooking kind
- 1 Tablespoon soy sauce

Directions

Combine all ingredients into the crockpot, cover and cook on low for 8 hours.

Mama's Meatloaf

Nutrition Information

Per Serving: 428 calories, 19g fat (4g saturated fat), 126mg cholesterol, 1040mg sodium, 45g carbohydrate 20g sugars, 6g fiber), 20g protein

Ingredients

- 1-pound ground round or chuck beef
- 1/2 cup ketchup
- ½ cup diced onion
- 1 cup crackers, I use the buttery flavored ones, crushed
- ½ cup chopped green chilies
- 1 egg
- ½ cup bell pepper, chopped (optional)
- 1 tsp garlic salt

Directions

Combine all ingredients and press firmly into the crockpot. Make a v shape in the top of the meatload and down the middle, I don't know exactly why but Mama always did it that way, and pour extra ketchup in the v. Cover the crockpot and cook on low for 8 hours.

Mississippi Pot Roast

Nutrition Information

Per Serving: 1171 calories, 79g fat (34g saturated
fat), 436mg cholesterol, 1562mg sodium, 4g carbohydrate
(0g sugars, 0g fiber), 100g protein

Ingredients

- 1 2-lb pot roast, frozen
- 1 package ranch dressing
- 1 stick real butter
- 6 whole pepperoncini peppers
- 1 package au jus mix
- DO NOT ADD WATER!

Directions

Place roast in the bottom of the crock pot. Sprinkle the 2
seasoning mixes over the top. Place the stick of butter on
top of the powdered seasonings. Place the peppers on top
and around the sides of the roast. Cook on low for 8 hours.
Serve with mashed potatoes or rice.

Spicy Barbecue Brisket

Per Serving: 869 calories, 53g fat (17g saturated fat), 221mg cholesterol, 2706mg sodium, 33g carbohydrate (21g sugars, 4g fiber), 62g protein

Ingredients

- 1 tablespoon finely chopped fresh oregano
- 1 tablespoon dark brown sugar
- 2 tablespoons olive oil
- 1 teaspoon ground cumin
- 3/4 teaspoon salt
- 1/2 teaspoon freshly ground black pepper
- 3 garlic cloves, grated or minced
- 1 pound trimmed beef brisket
- 2 medium tomatoes, chopped (about 2 cups)
- 1/2 medium onion, chopped (about 1 cup)
- 1 red bell pepper, chopped (about 1 cup)
- 1 can green chilies, chopped

Directions

Combine all the spices together into a rub. Rub the brisket on both sides, even poking the brisket with a fork so the meat will absorb more of the seasoning. Place the bell peppers and onion in the bottom of the crock pot with the tomatoes. Place the brisket on top. If there is any remaining rub, sprinkle it around the top. Cook on low for 8 hours. Remove the brisket from the crockpot and shred, returning to the crockpot before serving. Mix with the peppers, etc. and serve on tortillas with shredded cheese and sour cream.

Steak and Gravy

Nutrition Information

Per Serving: 399 calories, 8g fat (3g saturated fat), 128mg cholesterol, 830mg sodium, 15g carbohydrate (3g sugars, 1g fiber), 58g protein

Ingredients

- 2 large cubed steaks (10-oz)
- ¼ cup flour
- 1 chopped onion
- 2 cups beef broth1 can cream of celery soup
- ½ cup milk
- 1 package frozen broccoli and cauliflower
- 1 cup Velveeta cheese shreds
- 1 cup crushed Cheez-Its crackers
- Salt and pepper
- 1 tsp garlic salt

Directions

Place steaks in the bottom of the crockpot. Combine the rest of the ingredients, smoothing all lumps out of the flour, and pour over the steaks. Cook, covered, on low for 6-8 hours.

Serve over rice with corn for a quick and tasty meal.

Chapter 5

Chicken Main Dishes

Cheesy Chicken Broccoli Soup

Nutrition Information

Per Serving: 554 calories, 20g fat (9g saturated fat), 124mg cholesterol, 1718 mg sodium, 56g carbohydrate (7g sugars, 3g fiber), 38g protein

Ingredients

- 1 cup (100g), Broccoli, chopped and frozen
- 0.50 cup, shredded, Cheese, cheddar
- 1 container (1 3/10 cups ea.), Cream of Mushroom Soup
- 1 container (12.3 oz ea.), Chicken Breast canned, drained, or 1 cup cooked chicken breast
- 1 box Rice-A-Roni cheddar broccoli mix
- 3-4 cups water, depending on how thick you want the soup

Directions

Combine all ingredients except the shredded Cheddar cheese into the crockpot, cover and cook on low for 8 hours. Sprinkle the cheddar cheese across the soup when you serve.

Chicken Cacciatore

Nutrition Information

Per Serving: 390 calories, 15g fat (9g saturated fat), 99mg cholesterol, 674mg sodium, 37g carbohydrate (24g sugars, 7g fiber), 45g protein

Ingredients

- 2 chicken breasts or 2 chicken quarters
- 1 can Italian seasoned tomatoes
- 1 T Italian seasoning
- 1 onion cut in rings
- 1 cup fresh mushroom slices
- ½ bell pepper, sliced into strips
- 1 clove garlic, minced
- 1 small can tomato sauce
- ½ cup Parmesan cheese, for serving

Directions

Combine all ingredients into a crock-pot, stir to combine flavors. Cover and cook on low for 6-8 hours. Serve over spaghetti and sprinkle with shredded Parmesan cheese.

Chicken with Lemon Honey Glaze

Nutrition Information

Per Serving: 342 calories, 4g fat (1g saturated fat), 91mg cholesterol, 94mg sodium, 41g

Ingredients

- 2 frozen chicken breasts
- 1/4 cup lemon juice
- 1 cup chicken broth
- ½ Tablespoon minced garlic
- 1 Tablespoon cornstarch (to thicken the sauce)
- ¼ cup honey

Directions

Place the first four ingredients into the crockpot. Cover and cook on low for 8 hours.

Mix the cornstarch with 1 tablespoon cold water. When the mixture is smooth, stir it into the crockpot, continue stirring until the sauce is thickened. Slowly add the honey, except for 1 Tablespoon. Serve the chicken and sauce over rice, drizzle with the remaining honey.

Feta Chicken

Nutrition Information

Per Serving: 40 calories, 18g fat (6g saturated fat), 141mg cholesterol, 630mg sodium, 13g carbohydrate (5g sugars, 3g fiber), 45g protein

Ingredients

- 2 frozen chicken breasts
- ½ onion, sliced
- ½ green pepper, sliced thinly
- 2 Tablespoons minced garlic
- 1 can diced tomatoes or 3 fresh chopped tomatoes
- 1 small can sliced black olives
- ½ cup assorted olive tapenade (recipe underneath)
- salt and pepper to taste
- 1/4 cup crumbled feta

Directions

Combine all ingredients in the crockpot EXCEPT the feta cheese and olive tapenade. Cook, covered, on low for 6-8 hours.

To Serve: Place chicken and sauce aside garlic potatoes and green beans. Scoop the olive tapenade atop the chicken, then sprinkle with the feta cheese.

Olive Tapenade

- 1 cup pitted mixed olives
- 1 Tablespoon garlic, minced
- 1 Tablespoon capers
- 1 Tablespoon chopped fresh basil
- 1 tablespoon lemon juice
- 1 Tablespoon olive oil

Coarsely chop or blend all ingredients and chill before serving. (I like texture so I chop)

Garlic Chicken and Potatoes

Nutrition Information

Per Serving: 325 calories, 7g fat (0g saturated fat), 92mg cholesterol, 528mg sodium, 39g carbohydrate (6g sugars, 7g fiber), 28g protein

Ingredients

- 4-6 boneless chicken thighs, skinless -frozen
- 2 Tablespoons minced garlic
- 3 whole potatoes
- 10-ounces baby carrots
- 1 teaspoon olive oil
- ½ teaspoon paprika
- ¼ teaspoon black pepper
- 1 medium sliced onion

Directions

Place the onion slices in the bottom of the crockpot. Quarter the potatoes and place on top. Mix the olive oil, garlic, paprika and black pepper and smear on top of the chicken. Place over the potatoes. Place carrots on top. Cover and cook for 8 hours on low. Placing a paper towel or dishcloth under the lid of the crockpot will reduce the moisture in the dish and make it taste roasted.

Greek Inspired Chicken Asparagus Soup

Nutrition Information

Per Serving: 419 calories, 4g fat (1g saturated fat), 96mg cholesterol, 213mg sodium, 40g carbohydrate (7g sugars, 5g fiber), 48g protein

Ingredients

- 2 frozen chicken breasts
- ½ cup wild rice
- 2 Tablespoons lemon juice
- 1 10-ounce frozen package asparagus cuts
- 2 cups chicken broth
- 1 teaspoon minced garlic
- 1 teaspoon Greek seasoning
- Salt and pepper to taste

Directions

Place all the ingredients in a crockpot and cover. Cook on low for 8 hours. Before serving, remove the chicken breast(s) and shred. Place the chicken back into the pot and serve.

Italian Chicken with Green Beans and Potatoes

Nutrition Information

Per Serving: 520 calories, 18g fat (3g saturated fat), 85mg cholesterol, 764mg sodium, 55g carbohydrate (13g sugars, 8g fiber), 37g protein

Ingredients

- 2 chicken breasts, frozen
- 2 cups whole green beans, fresh is best but frozen works
- 2 sliced potatoes, medium
- ½ cup Italian bottled dressing

Directions

Combine all ingredients into a crockpot, cover and cook 6-8 hours. Serve with garlic toast.

Lemon Caper Chicken

Nutrition Information

Per Serving: 332 calories, 13g fat (5g saturated fat), 124mg cholesterol, 576mg sodium, 7g carbohydrate (2g sugars, 1g fiber), 38g protein

Ingredients

- 2 small lemons, sliced thinly
- 1 1/2 teaspoons sugar
- 4 garlic cloves, minced
- 2 larger skinless, boneless chicken breasts, frozen
- 1/2 teaspoon salt
- 1/2 teaspoon black pepper
- 1 tablespoon olive oil
- 2 tablespoons butter
- 1/2 cup dry white wine
- 1 cup chicken broth
- ¼ teaspoon oregano
- ¼ teaspoon thyme
- 1 teaspoon corn starch
- 2 tablespoons capers, rinsed and drained

Directions

Combine all the liquid ingredients and spices, except the capers. Place some of the lemon slices in the bottom of the crockpot and reserve the remaining for the top of the chicken. Place the chicken on top of the lemon slices. Pour the liquid with the spices on top. Reserve the capers for serving. Cook on low for 8 hours, covered. Before serving, remove the chicken from the crockpot. Make a slurry with the cornstarch and stir into the sauce. Stir until thickened. Place the chicken on a bed of rice. Pour the lemon sauce over the chicken and garnish with the capers. It makes a beautiful presentation with a spinach and purple onion salad.

Salsa Chicken

Nutrition Information

Per Serving: 359 calories, 14g fat (7g saturated fat), 93mg cholesterol, 1306mg sodium, 16g carbohydrate (9g sugars, 2g fiber), 43g protein

Ingredients

- 2 chicken breasts, frozen
- 1 cup salsa
- 1 package taco seasoning mix
- ½ cup shredded cheddar cheese
- 1 cup plain Greek yogurt
- Sliced black olives for garnish

Directions

Place chicken in the crockpot, sprinkle with the taco seasoning mix. Pour the salsa over the chicken and cook on low for 6-8 hours. When ready to serve, remove the chicken gently from the pot, stir in the Greek yogurt. To serve, place the chicken on the plate or over cooked rice, pour the sauce over the chicken. Sprinkle with cheese, then top with black olive slices.

This is delicious with rice and guacamole salad.

Sour Cream Chicken Enchiladas

Nutrition Information

Per Serving: 742 calories, 34g fat (16g saturated
fat), 130mg cholesterol, 2242mg sodium, 57g
carbohydrate (13g sugars, 9g fiber), 54g protein

Ingredients

- 5 corn tortillas, cut into six wedges each (like a
  pie)
- 1 cup shredded chicken, already cooked
- 1 cup shredded cheddar cheese
- 1 cup plain Greek yogurt
- 1 can green chilies (1/2 c), chopped
- 1 can cream of chicken soup
- 1 cup mild green salsa
- *Garnish*
- ½ cup shredded cheddar cheese
- ¼ cup sliced black olives
- Grape tomatoes, halved (1/2 cup)

Directions

Slice the tortillas into 6 pieces each, place in a bowl along
with all ingredients but the garnishes. Mix slowly to not
blend the ingredients. Place in a buttered crockpot and
cover, placing a paper towel under the lid. Cook on low for
6-8 hours. Before serving, sprinkle with the grated cheese

and olives. Place the tomatoes on top or along the side for bright color. Delicious with Spanish rice and guacamole.

Tomato Alfredo Chicken

Nutrition Information

Per Serving: 448 calories, 26g fat (8g saturated fat), 115mg cholesterol, 1442mg sodium, 24g carbohydrate (15g sugars, 4g fiber), 27g protein

Ingredients

- 2 frozen chicken breasts
- 1/2 jar Ragu Alfredo Sauce (any brand will do)
- 1 can diced tomatoes with Italian seasonings
- ½ tsp minced garlic
- 1 Roma tomato, sliced, for garnish
- 1 cup coarsely chopped fresh spinach leaves, washed and trimmed

Directions

Place all ingredients into the crockpot (except the Roma tomato) and turn on low. Cover and cook for 6-8 hours. Serve with fettucine noodles, top with the slices of Roma tomato.

Chapter 6   Pork Main Dishes

Carnita Pork

Nutrition Information

Per Serving: 555 calories, 26g fat (8g saturated fat), 195mg cholesterol, 1102mg sodium, 9g carbohydrate (3g sugars, 2g fiber), 66g protein

Ingredients

- 2 teaspoons olive oil
- 1 (1 1/2-pound) lean boneless pork roast, excess fat trimmed, cut into 3-inch chunks
- 1 cup chicken broth or Mexican beer
- 1 medium white onion, diced
- 2 Tablespoons garlic, minced
- 1 teaspoon cumin
- 1/2 teaspoon chili powder
- 1/2 teaspoons salt
- 1 Tablespoon lime juice
- ¼ cup medium salsa (or hot)

Directions

Mix all ingredients together in the crockpot, cover and cook for 8 hours on low. Shred with fork in crockpot, stir and serve.

If you want the pork to be crisp, place the ingredients on a cookie sheet and broil to desired crispness before serving. Pour ½ cup of the cooking liquid over the pork to flavor and keep from being dry.

Cheery Cherry Pork Loin

Nutrition Information

Per Serving: 677 calories, 8g fat (2g saturated fat), 6mg cholesterol, 1451mg sodium, 90g carbohydrate (5g sugars, 2g fiber), 54g protein

Ingredients

- 1 small pork loin 1 lbs. or so
- ½ cup chicken broth
- 1 can cherry pie filling
- Teriyaki sauce, about 1/4 cup

Directions

Poke the pork loin with a fork. Place in the bottom of a greased crockpot and pour Teriyaki sauce over the top Pour the can of cherry pie filling over the pork loin. Add ½ cup chicken broth. Cover and cook for 6-8 hours on low.

Corny Pork Chops

Nutrition Information

Calories 410 Calories from Fat 130 Total Fat 14g Saturated
Fat 3 1/2g Cholesterol 105mg Sodium 1180mg Total
Carbohydrate 40g Dietary Fiber 3g Sugars 5g Protein 32g

Ingredients

- 2 large pork chops
- 1 cup Southern Fried Corn (or sweet shoe peg corn)
- 2 cups cornbread stuffing mix or crumbled corn bread
- 1 tsp sage
- 1/4 cup chopped onion
- 1 1/2 cups chicken broth
- 1 whisked egg
- Salt and pepper to taste

Directions

Mix together the stuffing ingredients with the corn and
place in the bottom of a buttered crockpot. Place the pork
chops on top. Cover and cook 6-8 hours on low. Delicious
with a little extra sprinkle of black pepper.

Green Beans, Potatoes and Polish Sausage

Nutrition Information

Per Serving: 224 calories, 17g fat (6g saturated fat), 40mg cholesterol, 504mg sodium, 10g carbohydrate (4g sugars, 3g fiber), 10g protein

Ingredients

- 1/2 pound fresh green beans, snapped
- 1 onion sliced
- 4 potatoes
- ½ polish sausage, sliced in 4 pieces

Directions

Place all ingredients in the crockpot. Cover and cook on low for 6-8 hours.

Ham and Scalloped Potatoes

Nutrition Information

Per Serving: 618 calories, 20g fat (4g saturated fat), 90mg cholesterol, 1926mg sodium, 74g carbohydrate (8g sugars, 6g fiber), 34g protein

Ingredients

- 1 can Cream of Mushroom Condensed Soup
- 0.50 tsp paprika
- 0.25 tsp ground Pepper
- 1 cup sliced Onions
- 0.50 cup Fully Cooked Boneless Ham, sliced or diced
- 1.50 lb(s), Potato sliced (about 5 medium)
- 4 ounces Shredded Cheddar Cheese, reserve 1 ounce

Directions

Grease the crockpot. Mix the soup, paprika, cheese and pepper in a bowl. Layer the ingredients starting with the potatoes, onions, ham and sauce/soup. Cover and cook for 8 hours on low. Sprinkle with remaining cheese and serve.

Holiday Ham

Nutrition Information

Per Serving: 861 calories, 29g fat (10g saturated
fat), 194mg cholesterol, 4452mg sodium, 91g carbohydrate
(71g sugars, 5g fiber), 57g protein

Ingredients

- 2 or 3- pound bone in pre-cooked ham (it is
  easiest to buy a 5-6 pound ham and ask the
  butcher to slice in half, then freeze both portions)
- ½ cup brown sugar
- 1 cup pineapple juice
- ¼ cup real maple syrup

Directions

Rub all of the ham with the brown sugar, then place bone
side down in the crock pot. Combine the pineapple juice
and the syrup and pour over the ham. Cover and cook on
low for 6-8 hours. Serve with pineapple and cottage cheese
salads to enhance the pineapple flavor.

Pineapple Cottage Cheese Salads

Place a pineapple ring on a lettuce leaf. Top with scoop of
cottage cheese and a cherry.

Mr. B's Pork Chops

Nutrition Information

Per Serving: 638 calories, 24g fat (7g saturated fat), 121mg cholesterol, 1473mg sodium, 46g carbohydrate (9g sugars, 4g fiber), 63g protein

Ingredients

- 4 4-ounce pork chops or 2 8-ounce, frozen
- 1 cup plain Greek yogurt
- 1 can cream of chicken soup
- 1 can or 1 ½ cups whole green beans
- 2 cups frozen crinkle cut French fries
- Salt and pepper

Directions

Salt and pepper the pork chops on both sides. Grease the crockpot or spray. Mix together everything but the pork chops and place into the crockpot. Place the pork chops on top and cook, covered, on low for 6-8 hours. Great with crusty rolls and butter.

Pernil Pork

Nutrition Information

Per Serving: 504 calories, 21g fat (7g saturated fat), 226mg cholesterol, 1326mg sodium, 5g carbohydrate (0g sugars, 1g fiber), 70g protein

Ingredients

- 1 ½ lbs. pork tenderloin
- 2 Tablespoons minced garlic
- 2 Tablespoons lime juice
- 1 teaspoon black pepper
- 1 teaspoon olive oil
- 1 teaspoon white wine vinegar
- 1 teaspoon oregano
- 1 teaspoon chili pepper
- 1 teaspoon salt

Directions

Make a rub with everything but the pork tenderloin and rub all over the meat. Place in the crockpot and roast for 8 hours on low. DO NOT ADD LIQUID.

This is an amazing Puerto Rican dish to serve with black beans and rice. Garnish with quartered limes.

Smothered Pork Chops

Nutrition Information

Per Serving: 826 calories, 16g fat (4g saturated fat), 111mg cholesterol, 2623mg sodium, 77g carbohydrate (7g sugars, 4g fiber), 61g protein

Ingredients

- 2 large boneless pork chops, frozen (the nutrition info is for 16 oz total)
- 1 can golden mushroom soup
- ½ cup chicken broth or bullion
- 1 onion, sliced in circles very thinly
- 1 package instant stuffing mix, any flavor (I use the cornbread always)

Directions

Place the pork chops in the bottom of the crockpot. Place the onion rings on top. Next, mix the soup and broth or bullion and pour over the chops and onions. Lastly, sprinkle with the dry stuffing mix. Cook on low for 6-8 hours, covered. These chops will be tender but will have a crunchy topping.

Texas Boil

Nutrition Information

Per Serving: 751 calories, 20g fat (6g saturated fat), 525mg cholesterol, 1008mg sodium, 69g carbohydrate (7g sugars, 10g fiber), 70g protein

Ingredients

- 1/4 pound Cajun flavored smoked sausage
- 1 onion, quartered
- 1-2 Tablespoons shrimp boil
- 2 small cobs of corn
- 4 small potatoes
- 1 lb shrimp, raw
- 1 bay leaf
- 2 lemons halved
- 1 teaspoon minced garlic
- 1 stalk celery, cut in 4 pieces

Directions

Place everything except the shrimp in the crockpot and cook, covered, on low for 6-8 hours. Place the shrimp in the crockpot for the last 30 minutes before serving. Cover and cook 30 more minutes on low. Discard bay leaf and serve. Squeeze the lemons on top of the shrimp.

Chapter 7   Vegetarian Main Dishes

Chunky Tomato Tortellini Soup

Nutrition Information

Per Serving: 321 calories, 5g fat (2g saturated fat), 20mg cholesterol, 941mg sodium, 44g carbohydrate (15g sugars, 6g fiber), 21g protein

Ingredients

- 1 large can Italian diced tomatoes with basil and garlic
- 1 can vegetable broth
- 1 diced onion
- 3 Tablespoons minced garlic
- 2 Roma tomatoes, diced and set aside for garnish
- Salt and pepper
- 2 bay leaves
- 1 cup tortellini with pesto filling (Trader Joe's has it) or cheese filled

Directions

Combine all ingredients and cook, covered, on low for 8 hours. Remove bay leaves and serve with diced Roma tomatoes on top.

If you desire the tortellini *al dente*, add to soup 30 minutes before serving. Serve with toasted bread.

Lasagna

Nutrition Information

Per Serving: 569 calories, 19g fat (8g saturated fat), 55mg cholesterol, 1796mg sodium, 67g carbohydrate (30g sugars, 6g fiber), 36g protein

Ingredients

- 1 cup, Spinach - Raw
- 8 ounces Lowfat Cottage Cheese
- 1 cup shredded Mozzarella
- 2 cups Chunky Pasta Sauce
- ¼ cup Parmesan cheese, grated (save for serving)
- 3 lasagna noodles

Directions

Spray or butter your crockpot. Mix together the spinach, mozzarella cheese, and cottage cheese. Break the noodles into 3 or 4 pieces each, whichever fits in your crockpot.

Layer as following: Noodles, cheese mixture, pasta sauce. Reserve the Parmesan cheese for serving. Cover and cook on low for 8 hours. Will not be pretty but will be pretty tasty.

Minestrone Soup

Nutrition Information

Per Serving: 411 calories, 1g fat (0g saturated fat), 0mg cholesterol, 1230mg sodium, 86g carbohydrate (26g sugars, 21g fiber), 18g protein

Ingredients

- 1 sweet onion, diced
- 3 tablespoons garlic, minced
- 1 cup diced or shredded carrots, fresh
- 1 (12 ounce) can diced tomatoes with Italian seasoning
- 1 (15 ounce) can of cannellini beans, drained and rinsed
- 2 cups low-sodium vegetable stock
- 1 cup water
- 4 ounces of uncooked tiny pasta
- 12 asparagus spears, cut into thirds
- 1/2 cup of frozen sweet peas
- 1 cup of fresh spinach, stemmed and chopped
- salt and pepper to taste

Directions

Combine all ingredients except the pasta and asparagus in the crockpot, cover and cook on low for 8 hours, add the asparagus and pasta 30 minutes before serving. Serve with crusty bread.

Marinara Sauce

Nutrition Information

Per Serving: 219 calories, 4g fat (1g saturated fat), 0mg cholesterol, 2441mg sodium, 39g carbohydrate (20g sugars, 9g fiber), 11g protein

Ingredients

- 1 zucchini, chopped
- 1 onion, chopped
- 1 28-oz can whole tomatoes
- 1 small can tomato paste
- 2 Tablespoons minced garlic
- 1 teaspoon olive oil
- 1 teaspoon oregano
- ½ teaspoon basil
- 1 Tablespoon onion salt
- 2 cups spinach, chopped
- 1 Tablespoon red pepper flakes

Directions

Combine all ingredients in the crockpot, cover and cook on low for 8 hours.

Mushroom Stroganoff

Nutrition Information

Per Serving: 79 calories, 0g fat (0g saturated fat), 0mg cholesterol, 0mg sodium, 5g carbohydrate (3g sugars, 1g fiber), 8g protein

Ingredients

- 1 ½ pounds fresh mushrooms, chopped
- 3 tablespoons minced garlic
- 1 onion, thinly sliced
- 1 cup vegetable broth or vegetable stock
- 2 tsp smoked paprika
- Salt and Black pepper
- 4 tablespoons fresh parsley, chopped-for garnish on top
- 2 Tablespoons sour cream

Directions

Combine all ingredients in the crock pot and cover, cook on low for 8 hours. Stir in sour cream (2 tablespoons) right before serving. Serve over rice. Garnish with fresh parsley.

Spicy Special Vegetable Soup

Nutrition Information

Per Serving: 302 calories, 3g fat (0g saturated fat), 0mg cholesterol, 874mg sodium, 63g carbohydrate (17g sugars, 7g fiber), 7g protein

Ingredients

- 1 pkg Birds Eye Baby Mixed Beans and Carrots, coarsely chopped (16 oz.)
- 1 8oz can spicy V-8 juice
- 1 can diced tomatoes with basil and garlic
- 2 diced potatoes
- 1 diced onion
- 1 pkg Birds Eye Fiesta Lime Corn (10 ounces)
- 3 c water

Directions

Combine all ingredients in the crock pot and cover, cook on low for 8 hours. Serve with tortilla chips.

Stuffed Bell Peppers

Nutrition Information

Per Serving: 332 calories, 4g fat (1g saturated fat), 0mg cholesterol, 934mg sodium, 75g carbohydrate (14g sugars, 17g fiber), 17g protein

Ingredients

- 3 bell peppers, topped, cleaned and seeded, ready to stuff
- 1/2 cup uncooked brown rice, rinsed
- 1 14-ounce can black beans, rinsed and drained AND 1 can refried beans, combined and HALVED, (save the other half for burritos)
- 3/4 cups red enchilada sauce
- 1/2 teaspoon cumin
- 1/2 teaspoon chili powder
- 1/2 teaspoon onion powder
- 1/4 teaspoon garlic salt
- Black pepper
- Cilantro, chopped, to taste
- ¼ cup shredded cheddar cheese

Directions

Combine all stuffing ingredients. Place the bell peppers into the bottom of the crockpot. Pour in 1 inch of water. Place stuffing ingredients into the peppers. Cover and cook on low for 8 hours. Serve with diced avocados and shredded cheese on top.

Sweet Potato Soup (Savory)

Nutrition Information

Per Serving: 221 calories, 1g fat (0g saturated fat), 0mg cholesterol, 333mg sodium, 29g carbohydrate (10g sugars, 6g fiber), 20g protein

Ingredients

- 3 cups vegetable broth
- 2 med sweet potatoes, peeled and shredded
- 1/2 cup chopped onion
- 1 stalks of celery, chopped
- 2 tablespoons chopped garlic
- 1 cup almond milk, unsweetened
- 1/2 tsp tarragon
- 2 cups baby spinach, chopped

Directions

Place all ingredients into the crockpot. Cover and cook on low for 6-8 hours. Before serving, whip with immersion blender or smash with a potato masher if pieces are thicker than your liking.

Thai Broccoli Bowl with Peanut-Lime Dressing

Nutrition Information

Per Serving: 27 calories, 0g fat (0g saturated fat), 0mg cholesterol, 38mg sodium, 3g carbohydrate (2g sugars, 3g fiber), 1g protein

Ingredients

- 1 spaghetti squash
- 2 cups steamed broccoli
- 2 cups water
- 1 can water chestnuts, drained
- Red pepper flakes, to taste

Directions

Poke holes all over the spaghetti squash with a fork. Place into a crockpot and pour the 2 cups of water over it. Cover and cook on low for 8 hours.

To serve:

Mix together the dressing. Slice the squash in half and separate the strings, discard the seeds. Place the squash, water chestnuts, and broccoli into a bowl. Drizzle with the peanut dressing and red pepper flakes, if desired.

Peanut Lime Dressing

Nutrition Information   Per Serving: 407 calories, 32g fat (5g saturated fat), 0mg cholesterol, 328mg sodium, 23g carbohydrate (12g sugars, 4g fiber), 14g protein

Ingredients

- ½ cup smooth peanut butter
- 2 tablespoons lime juice
- 1 tablespoon sugar
- 1 teaspoon reduced-sodium soy sauce

Whisk together, adding water to thin to desired consistency.

Three Bean as Hot as You Like Chili

Nutrition Information

This recipe is 4 servings.

Per Serving: 435 calories, 8g fat (1g saturated fat), 0mg cholesterol, 1947mg sodium, 73g carbohydrate (10g sugars, 22g fiber), 10g protein

Ingredients

- 1 can black beans, rinsed and drained
- 1 can pinto beans, rinsed and drained
- 1 can garbanzo beans, rinsed and drained
- 1 can Rotel tomatoes, as hot as you like
- 3 cups vegetable broth
- ½ cup red and green peppers, chopped
- ½ cup onion, chopped
- 1 pkg chili seasoning mix
- 1 avocado, diced for garnish

Directions

Combine in crockpot, cover and cook on low for 8 hours, serve with diced avocado on top. Great with tortilla chips.

Chapter 8   Vegetable Side Dishes

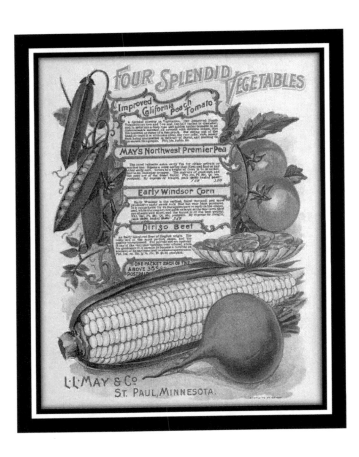

Baked Beans

Nutrition Information

Per Serving: 591 calories, 4g fat (0g saturated fat), 0mg cholesterol, 1542mg sodium, 119g carbohydrate (51g sugars, 20g fiber), 23g protein

Ingredients

- 1 cup Great Northern Beans
- ½ cup chopped onion
- 3 cups water
- ¼ cup brown sugar
- ¼ cup molasses
- ¼ cup ketchup
- 1 tsp salt
- 2 Tablespoons mustard (French's)
- 2 bacon slices, raw, chopped

Directions

Combine all ingredients in the crockpot, cover and cook on low for 8 hours.

Serve with crusty bread for sopping.

Broccoli Cauliflower Casserole

Nutrition Information

Per Serving: 489 calories, 28g fat (10g saturated fat), 62mg cholesterol, 514mg sodium, 44g carbohydrate (19g sugars, 3g fiber), 19g protein

Ingredients

- 1 can cream of celery soup
- ½ cup milk
- 1 package frozen broccoli and cauliflower
- 1 cup Velveeta cheese shreds
- 1 cup crushed Cheez-Its crackers
- Salt and pepper

Directions

Combine all ingredients into a buttered crockpot and cook, covered, for 8 hours on low.

Company Carrots

Nutrition Information

Per Serving: 327 calories, 18g fat (12g saturated fat), 50mg cholesterol, 499mg sodium, 28g carbohydrate (15g sugars, 7g fiber), 12g protein

Ingredients

- 1 pound carrots, sliced into coins
- 2 T Thyme
- 3 T butter
- 1 cup plain Greek yogurt
- ½ cup chicken broth

Directions

Combine all ingredients except the sour cream into the crockpot. Place on low and cook for 6-8 hours, covered. Mash the carrots with a potato masher. Before serving, stir in the sour cream to coat the carrots. They should be moist and soft and resemble mashed potatoes.

Creamed Corn

Nutrition Information

Per Serving: 548 calories, 44g fat (27g saturated fat), 126mg cholesterol, 348mg sodium, 34g carbohydrate (8g sugars, 3g fiber), 10g protein

Ingredients

- 2 cups frozen corn
- 4 ounces cream cheese
- ¼ cup butter
- ¼ cup milk
- 1 teaspoon sugar
- Salt and pepper

Directions

Slice the cream cheese into smaller chunks. Combine all ingredients into the crockpot and cover, cook for 8 hours on low.

Fiesta Lime Corn

Nutrition Information

Per Serving: 240 calories, 12g fat (7g saturated fat), 31mg cholesterol, 86mg sodium, 33g carbohydrate (5g sugars, 5g fiber), 5g protein

Ingredients

- 2 cups frozen corn
- ½ cup lime juice
- 1 teaspoon cumin
- 2 Tablespoons butter
- ½ teaspoon onion salt
- ¼ teaspoon chili powder, more to taste if you like it more spicy
- Sprinkle of red pepper flakes

Directions

Place all in the crockpot and cook, covered, on low for 8 hours.

French Onion Soup

Nutrition Information

Per Serving: 507 calories, 29g fat (15g saturated fat), 74mg cholesterol, 2661mg sodium, 34g carbohydrate (2g sugars, 1g fiber), 20g protein

Ingredients

- 2 yellow onions, sliced and separated into rings
- 3 cups beef broth
- 3 Tablespoons butter
- 1 Tablespoon minced garlic
- ½ teaspoon salt
- ¼ cup cooking sherry
- 1 bay leaf
- ¼ cup shredded parmesan
- 4 slices French bread
- ¼ cup shredded Gruyere cheese
- ¼ cup shredded Mozzarella cheese

Directions

Combine all the ingredients until you get to the cheeses into the crockpot. Cover and cook on low for 8 hours. Before serving, toast the French bread. Ladle the soup into oven-safe bowls, place bread on top of the soup, and place cheese on top of the toasted bread. Broil until cheese is bubbly.

German Potato Salad

Nutrition Information

Per Serving: 264 calories, 9g fat (2g saturated fat), 12mg cholesterol, 1010mg sodium, 40g carbohydrate (7g sugars, 4g fiber), 6g protein

Ingredients

- 2 cups quartered or sliced potatoes
- ¼ c water
- ½ T vinegar
- ½ T sugar
- 3 bacon slices, cooked and crumbled
- 1 can cream of chicken soup
- ½ c onion
- 4 T fresh parsley, chopped for garnish
- 1 bacon slice, crumbled, for garnish

Directions

Combine all ingredients in the crockpot, stir once to blend flavors. Cover and cook on low for 8 hours. Add the chopped parsley. Serve with the crumbled bacon on top.

Green Beans (Haricots Verts a la Provençale)

Nutrition Information

Per Serving: 428 calories, 28g fat (17g saturated fat), 297mg cholesterol, 953mg sodium, 15g carbohydrate (5g sugars, 2g fiber), 29g protein

Ingredients

- 1 lbs. whole green beans, fresh
- 1 clove garlic, minced
- 1 can fresh tomatoes, diced
- 1 T thyme
- ½ cup diced onion
- 1 bay leaf
- 2 cloves
- Sprinkle of parsley to serve

Directions

Place all ingredients in a 2-quart crockpot and place on low. Stir once to blend the seasonings. Cook, covered, for 6-8 hours. Before serving, sprinkle with chopped fresh parsley. You can fish out the cloves and bay leaf or leave them in, your choice.

Southern Potatoes and Pepper Gravy

Nutrition Information

Per Serving: 566 calories, 3g fat (17g saturated fat), 89mg cholesterol, 680mg sodium, 56g carbohydrate (10g sugars, 5g fiber), 13g protein

Ingredients

- 1 pound Yukon Gold potatoes, sliced
- 6 ounces evaporated milk
- 2 tsp butter
- ¼ cup water
- 4-ounces cream cheese, cut in small pieces
- 1 package peppered gravy mix

Directions

Butter the crockpot. Slice potatoes and place in crockpot. Pour the milk over the potatoes. Add the small pieces of cream cheese on top, then the butter. Mix the gravy mix with the water until well blended. Pour on top of the other ingredients. Cover, placing a paper towel under the lid. Cook on low for 8 hours. Stir before serving.

White Saucy Spinach

Nutrition Information

Per Serving: 383 calories, 29g fat (17g saturated fat), 252mg cholesterol, 761mg sodium, 8g carbohydrate (5g sugars, 1g fiber), 23g protein

Ingredients

- 3 cups spinach, chopped
- 1 cup cottage cheese
- ¼ cup butter, melted
- 2 eggs, beaten
- ½ teaspoon nutmeg
- ¼ cup flour
- ¼ cup milk
- ½ teaspoon salt

Directions

Combine the eggs and butter and nutmeg, then add the cottage cheese, then the spinach. Combine the flour and milk until no lumps are in the slurry, stir well into the spinach mixture. Place into a buttered crockpot, cover. Place a paper towel under the lid to remove condensation while cooking. Cook on low setting for 8 hours.

Zucchini Casserole

Nutrition Information

Per Serving: 484 calories, 35g fat (18g saturated fat), 70mg cholesterol, 532mg sodium, 30g carbohydrate (5g sugars, 3g fiber), 14g protein

Ingredients

- 4 zucchini squash, sliced thinly into rounds (about 4 cups)
- 1 cup crushed Chicken-in-a-Biscuit brand crackers
- 1 T butter
- 2 T minced onion
- Salt and pepper to taste
- ½ cup sour cream
- ½ cup shredded cheddar cheese, separated in 2 servings

Directions

Butter or grease a crockpot. Place all ingredients inside except ¼ cup cheddar cheese. Stir the ingredients, cover, placing a paper towel under the lid of the crockpot. Cook for 6-8 hours on low. Before serving, remove cover and sprinkle with remaining cheese. Replace cover until cheese is melted.

Chapter 9   Breads and Desserts

Apple Brown Betty

Nutrition Information

Per Serving: 573 calories, 13g fat (7g saturated fat), 31mg cholesterol, 179mg sodium, 119g carbohydrate (102g sugars, 6g fiber), 2g protein

Ingredients

- 2 chopped apples, I prefer Gala
- ½ cup brown sugar
- ¼ cup white sugar
- ½ teaspoon cinnamon
- Dash of Salt
- 1/3 cup oats
- 1/3 cup brown sugar
- 2 Tablespoons butter
- Raisins (if desired)
- ½ teaspoon vanilla

Directions

Mix the apples, brown and white sugars, salt and cinnamon to coat the apples evenly. Place the apple mixture in the bottom of the liberally buttered crockpot. Combine the oats, 1/3 c brown sugar, butter, raisins and vanilla together, mixture will be coarse. Sprinkle this on top of the apples. Cover and cook 8 hours on low.

Apple Pie Cobbler

Nutrition Information

Per Serving: 650 calories, 32g fat (6g saturated fat), 31mg cholesterol, 179mg sodium, 88g carbohydrate (51g sugars, 6g fiber), 6g protein

Ingredients

- 2 apples, peeled and chopped
- ½ cup sugar
- 1 cup biscuit mix
- ¾ cup milk
- 1 tsp cinnamon
- 1 tsp vanilla
- ¼ cup real butter
- ½ cup apple juice or water

Directions

Combine apples, vanilla, cinnamon, water in the bottom of a buttered crockpot. Mix together the biscuit mix, and milk. Pour on top of the apples. Melt the butter and pour over the biscuit mix. Cover and cook on low for 8 hours.

Black Forest Brownies

Nutrition Information

Per Serving: 1060 calories, 18g fat (7g saturated fat), 0mg cholesterol, 533mg sodium, 181g carbohydrate (68g sugars, 3g fiber), 6g protein

Ingredients

- 1 envelope brownie mix
- 1 can cherry pie filling
- 2 tablespoons Chocolate chips

Directions

Butter the crockpot. Mix the brownie mix as directed, pour into crockpot. Pour in one can of cherry pie filling on top. Cover and cook on low for 8 hours. Place in serving bowls hot, sprinkle with choc chips.

If you place the chocolate chips in the crockpot, this will be a big mess to clean. (Ask me how I know this. ;-)

Bread Pudding with Berries

Nutrition Information

Per Serving: 337 calories, 9g fat (4g saturated fat), 176mg cholesterol, 203mg sodium, 54g carbohydrate (43g sugars, 3g fiber), 11g protein

Ingredients

- 2 cups bread cubes
- 1 cup whole milk
- 2 eggs
- 1 teaspoon vanilla extract
- 1 teaspoon cinnamon
- ¼ cup sugar
- 1 ½ cups fresh or frozen berries

Directions

Combine all ingredients except berries and bread cubes into a bowl and mix/whisk together. When smooth, pour over bread cubes and soak for 15 minutes. Butter the crockpot. After confirming the bread cubes are well coated, pour the berries gently over the bread mix and fold. Pour the entire mix into the crockpot. Cover and cook for 8 hours.

Serve with additional berries.

Chocolate Lava Cake with Chocolate Chip Icing

Nutrition Information

Per Serving: 845 calories, 29g fat (16g saturated fat), 15mg cholesterol, 1089mg sodium, 137g carbohydrate (96g sugars, 8g fiber), 13g protein

Ingredients

- 1 Martha White chocolate chip muffin mix, 7-ounce size
- 1 pkg chocolate pudding mix, 3.9-ounce size
- 2 cups milk
- ½ cup chocolate chips

Directions

Fix the muffin mix as directed and pour into a well buttered crockpot. Combine the pudding mix with the milk. Pour HALF into the crockpot. Pour the other half into a bowl and eat it. Pour the chocolate chips over the pudding. Do not stir anything. Cover and cook on low for 6-8 hours. Serve hot with vanilla ice cream and invite me over, please.

Easiest Peach Cobbler

Nutrition Information

Per Serving: 723 calories, 20g fat (7g saturated fat), 20mg cholesterol, 922mg sodium, 123g carbohydrate (72g sugars, 4g fiber), 7g protein

Ingredients

- 1 pkg Jiffy yellow cake mix
- 1 large can peaches with juice
- 3/4 stick real butter
- 1 tsp cinnamon
- ½ tsp nutmeg

Directions

Pour peaches into crockpot. Sprinkle with cinnamon and nutmeg. Sprinkle cake mix on top evenly. Melt butter in microwave and pour over the top of the cake mix. DO NOT STIR. Cover and cook for 8 hours on low.

Chapter 10   Tips and Tricks

This is a list of short cuts and cooking hints that I have learned by experience.

- You will notice that I use frozen meat in most of my recipes. I use this trick to save time and to keep the meat from losing texture while cooking for 8 hours. I have found that cooking fresh meat 8 hours can turn the meat into a tasty lump.

- To thicken a sauce that is HOT, combine 1 Tablespoon cornstarch with 1 Tablespoon COLD water, stir until it is smooth, and then stir it into the still bubbling sauce. Continue to stir until the sauce is the desired thickness.

- I use less seasoning in the recipe and more at the table. I know how to sprinkle at the plate but I haven't caught the knack of removing too much from the cook pot.

- To thicken a sauce with flour, mix 2 Tablespoons flour with ¼ COLD water. Make into a slurry (mix thoroughly) and pour slowly into the heated sauce, stirring continuously.

- To get the sale prices at the grocery store I often buy twice the size of whole meat I desire (like a ham or roast) and ask the butcher to cut it in half and wrap separately.

- I buy ground meat and cook it all with onions and bell peppers when I bring it home. I then package it in 1 cup increments in freezer bags, flattened as much as possible. I pull out the desired amount from the freezer to add to the crockpot.

- I cook whole chickens in the crockpot seasoned with paprika, salt, pepper, and garlic. These taste amazingly like rotisserie chicken. After we have eaten it for the first meal, I debone and coarsely chop. I place this also in freezer bags in one cup increments for later use.

- When I pull the already cooked meats from the freezer I add ¼ cup water and taco or fajita seasoning mix, stir in a skillet to combine while thawing, and serve burritos or tacos that night for supper.

Conclusion

Thank you for purchasing my book, **Crockpot Cooking for 2: Easy Dump and Go! Fix-It and Forget-It Recipes.**

I hope that you have enjoyed the recipes and found a new freedom from tedious cooking chores. It is my anticipation that you will find many favorites in this easy cookbook as I have listed my best recipes from my pantry. I wanted to share dinners that were delicious, fast, and stress-free for you.

If you found this book useful and informative, please write a review on Amazon.com.

Thank you,

Mary Criswell-Carpenter

www.marycriswellcarpenter.com

email: marycriswellcarpenter@outlook.com

Find my other books at

www.marycriswellcarpenter.com

or on Amazon at

https://www.amazon.com/-/e/B0153OZ868

Made in the USA
Middletown, DE
22 December 2023

46687854R00066